Hindu

Anita Ganeri

Children's Press
A Division of Grolier Publishing
New York London Hong Kong Sydney
Danbury, Connecticut

Library of Congress Cataloging-in-Publication
Data

Ganeri, Anita, 1961-
    Hindu / by Anita Ganeri.
        p. cm. — (Beliefs and Cultures)
    ISBN 0-516-08076-8
    1. Hinduism—Juvenile literature.
    [I. Hinduism.] I. Title. II Series.
    BL1203.G36 1995   94-47344
    294.5—dc20   CIP AC

©1996 Watts Books
First American Edition © 1996 by
Children's Press
A Division of Grolier Publishing
Sherman Turnpike
Danbury, Connecticut 06816
Printed in Great Britain
Published simultaneously in Canada

1 2 3 4 5 6 7 8 9 0 R 05 04 03 02 01 00 99 98
97 96

Series Editor: Sarah Ridley
Designer: Liz Black
Copy Editor: Nicola Barber
Picture Researchers: Brooks Krikler
Illustrators: pages 20-21 Piers Harper, pages 5
and 22 Aziz Khan
Photographer (activities): Steve Shott
Consultant: Geoff Teece

Photographs: Eye Ubiquitous 12b, 24, 29b, 30b; Robert
Harding Picture Library cover (left),14t, 22; Michael
Holford 5; Hutchison Library 25l, 30t; Bipinchandra Mistry
4t, 4b, 7, 11t, 11b, 14b, 16b, 18, 19, 28, 29t; Bury
Peerless 6, 25r; Frank Spooner Picture Library 23; Trip
cover (right), 8t, 8b, 10, 12t, 15t, 15b, 16t.

CONTENTS

Hinduism is one of the world's oldest living religions. Its followers are called *Hindus*, and they live mainly in India, where Hinduism began. Religion plays an extremely important part in the lives of Hindus. Religion governs how they live, what they eat, and how they view the world. In fact, Hindus do not call their religion "Hinduism." That name was invented by Western scholars in the 19th century. Hindus simply consider their faith to be *sanatana dharma* – the "eternal teaching," or "law." Hinduism is a colorful and lively faith, with many traditions and many ways of worship.

People gather in the temple to worship, make their offerings to the gods, consult the priests, and meet friends.

This is the sacred sound "OM," the symbol of goodness. It is often chanted to help people as they meditate.

HINDU BEGINNINGS

Hinduism developed gradually – it has no founder and no single sacred book. It began about 4,000 years ago at the time of the Indus Valley civilization in northwest India. Archaeologists have found Indus statues thought to show an early form of the great Hindu god, *Shiva*. In about 1500 B.C., people from central Asia, called Aryans, invaded northern India. They brought with them their own religious beliefs. Their ideas, over time, mixed with those of the people of the Indus Valley. Hindus still worship some of the Aryan gods, such as *Agni*, the god of fire, and read Aryan sacred texts, such as the *Rig Veda* (see page 18).

These ancient temples stand on the seashore at Mahabalipuram in South India. They are dedicated to Shiva.

Today, most Hindus live in India, but there are large Hindu communities in Nepal, the Middle East, Fiji, and Mauritius. Other Hindus live and work in parts of the world such as Britain, North America, Africa, Southeast Asia, and the Caribbean.

Hinduism began in India but has spread to many other parts of the world, wherever Hindus have settled.

SPOTLIGHT

- About eight out of ten of the people in India are Hindus.

- Worldwide, about 700 million people are Hindus.

- You have to be born a Hindu. You cannot become one.

HINDU POPULATION
- over 600 million
- 1 to 20 million
- 100,000 to 1 million
- 5,000 to 100,000

HINDU BELIEFS

Hinduism is a whole way of life, rather than just a set of religious beliefs. It can be practiced in many different ways. Some Hindus pray every day; others hardly ever pray. Saying prayers and visiting the temple are not necessary in Hinduism. Each person is free to worship in their own way. However, many Hindus share the same basic beliefs and values.

Hindus believe that when you die, your soul lives on and is reborn in another body – human or animal. This cycle of death and rebirth is called *samsara*. The quality of your next life depends on how you behave in this life. If you live a good life, you will be reborn in a higher form. If you live an evil life, you will be reborn in a lower form. This chain of actions and their effects is called *karma*.

Each village has its own small temple or shrine. It is often very simple, like this shrine underneath a tree. Villagers stop to worship here as they go about their daily lives.

The ultimate aim of a Hindu's life is to gain *moksha*, or salvation, and break free of the cycle of *samsara*. The higher you are born in each rebirth, the closer to *moksha* you are. Moksha is also seen as the time when your individual soul (*atman*) merges into the supreme spirit (*Brahman*).

These children are studying at a religious school, called an *ashram*. They are Brahmins from the highest Hindu caste.

THE CASTE SYSTEM

Hindu society has traditionally been divided into four main groups, called "castes." These are Brahmans (priests), *Kshatriyas* (nobles and soldiers), *Vaishyas* (traders), and *Sudras* (servants). Outside the caste system are people who do jobs considered dirty or menial, such as sweeping the streets. They used to be called "untouchables" but are now known as the "scheduled castes." In the past, the caste system was closely followed, and people of high and low castes never mixed. Today, the caste system is less strict, but it still affects people's lives.

INTERVIEW

The caste system does not really affect our lives in America. Traditional parents still try to find someone of the same caste for their daughter or son to marry. But we do not judge people by what caste they are.

Ramesh Chatterjee, age 55. New York, USA.

FOOD TASTES AND TABOOS

Many Hindus are vegetarians. They believe in the principle of *ahimsa*, or nonviolence. This principle forbids killing living beings, even for food. A typical Hindu vegetarian meal consists of rice or *chapatis* (rounds of flat bread), several spicy vegetable dishes, *dhal* (lentils), *dahi* (yogurt), and pickles. Hindus traditionally eat with their fingers, using their right hands. They consider their left hands to be unclean.

On festival days, people exchange gifts of homemade candy. The candy is made mainly of milk, nuts, and sugar.

To Hindus, cows are sacred animals. Most Hindus will not eat beef, even if they are not strict vegetarians.

In many Indian states, cows are never harmed or killed but are allowed to roam freely, even on traffic-filled streets.

MAKING CARROT HALVA

YOU WILL NEED (for 4 people):

- 1 pound grated carrots
- 1 tablespoon raisins
- 8 cardamon pods
- heavy saucepan
- Wooden spoon
- 3 cups milk
- 4 tablespoons sugar
- 3 tablespoons vegetable oil
- Nonstick frying pan
- Cream (optional)
- 1 tablespoon unsalted pistachio nuts, crushed

♣ Ask an adult for help with the cooking.

NOTE: If your local supermarket does not have all these ingredients, you can get them from any Asian food store.

WHAT TO DO:

1 Bring the carrots, cardamon pods, and milk to a boil in the saucepan. Lower the heat and simmer for about an hour, or until the liquid is gone, stirring regularly.

You can pick out the cardamon pods at this stage if you don't like their strong flavor.

2 Heat the oil in the frying pan and add the carrot mixture. Stir-fry for 10 minutes, stirring all the time.

3 Add the sugar, raisins, and crushed pistachio nuts. Stir-fry the mixture for another 2-3 minutes.

4 Spoon the halva into bowls and serve warm, with a spoonful of cream.

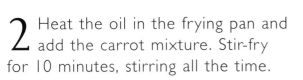

GODS AND GODDESSES

Most Hindus believe in a supreme spirit, called Brahman. But Hindus do not pray to Brahman as Christians pray to God, or Muslims to Allah. Hindus believe that hundreds of gods and goddesses represent different aspects of Brahman. Some Hindus worship many gods and goddesses. Some worship one specific divinity. Others do not worship any gods.

Hindu gods and goddesses are often shown with many heads or several arms, each holding a sacred object. These features symbolize their special powers and the aspect of Brahman that they represent.

Vishnu, the preserver and protector of the universe, and his wife, Lakshmi, the goddess of wealth and beauty

THE HINDU TRINITY

The three most important Hindu gods are *Brahma*, the creator; *Vishnu*, the preserver; and *Shiva*, the destroyer. Vishnu and Shiva are important gods, with many temples dedicated to them.

Brahma

Brahma, the first member of the Hindu trinity, is the creator of the universe. His statue has four heads, facing each of the four corners of the earth. He rides on a swan or sits on a sacred lotus blossom. His wife is the goddess of learning and the arts, *Saraswati*. Brahma has four hands, one always raised in blessing.

Vishnu

Vishnu is the preserver of the universe. He is often shown riding on an eagle or sleeping on a giant serpent. His wife is *Lakshmi*, goddess of beauty and wealth.

This statue shows Shiva, Lord of Dance. The circle of flame around him represents the never-ending cycle of time.

knowledge. Shiva rides on a huge bull, called *Nandi*. His wife is the goddess *Parvati*.

Rama and Krishna

Rama and *Krishna* are worshiped as gods all over India. Rama is the hero of the *Ramayana* poem – a long epic poem (see page 19) – and represents virtue and courage. Krishna is more mischievous and fond of performing miracles. He is a key figure in the *Bhagavad Gita*, which forms part of the *Mahabharata* poem (see page 19).

Shiva

Shiva is the destroyer of evil in the universe. He carries a trident, the symbol of destruction. On his forehead is the third eye of

Rama is one of the most popular of all Hindu gods. He is shown here with his wife, *Sita,* and the monkey-god, Hanuman.

SPOTLIGHT

Vishnu has visited the earth nine times to save the world from evil in times of trouble. He used the following disguises:

1 Matsya, the fish
2 Kurma, the tortoise
3 Varaha, the boar
4 Narasimha, the lion
5 Vamana, the dwarf
6 Parusha-Rama, the warrior
7 Rama, the ideal man
8 Krishna, the blue god
9 Buddha, the founder of Buddhism

Kalki, the 10th visit, is yet to come.

The power of the goddess

Parvati is often worshiped as the kind, gentle mother goddess. But in other forms she can be cruel and terrible. As *Durga*, the warrior goddess, she rides a tiger and holds a weapon in each of her ten hands. As the goddess *Kali*, she wears a skull necklace and conquers the ugliness of evil.

Ganesh

Ganesh, the elephant-headed god, is the son of Shiva and Parvati. He is one of the most popular Hindu gods. According to legend, Shiva cut off Ganesh's original human head in a rage and later replaced it with a wise elephant's head.

The gods once lent Durga their weapons and begged her to kill the terrible buffalo demon, Mahishasura.

Ganesh is worshiped as the god who solves difficulties. Hindus pray to him whenever they start something new — a new job, a new school, or moving to a new house.

Making a Ganesh elephant mask

You will need:

- gray cardboard
- pencil
- glue
- paint
- glitter
- elastic
- scissors
- paintbrush
- sequins or tinsel
- sticky tape

What to do:

1 Fold the cardboard in half and draw the shape of half an elephant's head on it. Cut out and complete with ears and eyeholes. Fold the ears so they stick out slightly.

2 Cut another piece of cardboard in the shape of the elephant's trunk. Shape the trunk so that it curls to one side.

3 Glue the trunk onto the inside of the head. Now decorate the mask. Paint dots around the eyes, or stick on tinsel or sequins. Sprinkle on some glitter. Make a hole at each side of the mask by the earfolds and thread a piece of elastic through.

Make sure the elastic is big enough to go around your head. Knot the ends through the holes.

WAYS OF WORSHIP

Many Hindus worship in temples dedicated to a particular god or goddess. The temple is seen as the god's home on earth, and a statue of the god stands in the innermost and most sacred part of the temple. There is no obligation for Hindus to visit the temple or to pray regularly, although a great many Hindus make a special visit on festival days or family occasions.

There are thousands of temples in India. Every town and village has its places of worship. Temples have also been built in other countries where Hindus have settled.

People visit small, roadside shrines on their way to work or school. They say a short prayer or leave an offering.

Everywhere, temples are gathering places for the whole community. They are happy places full of noise, color, and life.

WORSHIP AT HOME

Hindus also worship at home or at roadside shrines. Many Hindu homes have a room − or part of a room − set aside as a shrine with a statue or picture of their favorite god or goddess. The family uses the shrine for prayers, or *puja*, in the morning and evening. You take your shoes off before you approach the shrine, just as you would in a temple.

At home, the family shrine may be a whole room, part of a room, or simply a small closet or a shelf.

VISITING THE TEMPLE

There are no regular services in a Hindu temple, as there are in a Christian church, for example. People can visit whenever they like for puja and for *darshana* — a sight of a sacred image that symbolizes the presence of a god or goddess.

Everyone must take off their shoes before entering the temple. Then they walk clockwise round the main shrine, with their right hands toward the god. They bring *prasada* — offerings of fruit, candy, and flowers. The temple priest lays these offerings before the god to be blessed, then returns them to the worshipers to bestow the god's blessing upon

Every Hindu temple has a bell. You ring the bell as you enter the temple and again as you leave it.

them. With his finger, he marks the foreheads of the worshipers with the red *tilaka* (sign) of blessing. Worshipers also pass their hands over the sacred fire, then over their heads, as a form of blessing.

Outside every temple, there are stalls selling offerings for the gods, such as candy, incense, and garlands of flowers. The garlands are hung on the statue of the god or goddess inside the temple.

INTERVIEW

I go to the temple once a week with my mother and at special times such as the Diwali and Holi festivals. I also say my prayers every day in the small shrine room in my house. I like it best when the whole family joins in the puja and my parents tell us stories about the gods.
Nidhi Churiwala, age 13. Calcutta, India.

PRIESTS AND HOLY MEN

Each temple has its own Brahman priest. Priests visit people's homes to recite sacred texts and prepare horoscopes. Priests also perform special ceremonies such as weddings. In return, the priests are given food and money. *Sadhus* are holy men who have given up all their worldly goods to wander from place to place in search of enlightenment and salvation.

The horizontal marks on this sadhu's forehead show he is a follower of Shiva. Sadhus who follow Vishnu have three vertical marks on their foreheads.

The different positions or postures of yoga are called *asanas*. This yogi is sitting in the lotus position.

YOGA AND MEDITATION

Some holy men, and indeed, ordinary Hindus, use yoga and meditation to concentrate their minds in their search for moksha. Yoga is a system of exercises for both the mind and body. Yoga has become very popular all over the world. You learn to control your body through breathing and posture and to concentrate your mind through meditation. Hindu meditation may mean focusing one's thoughts on a special pattern called a *mandala*. Some people also meditate by repeating a special word or phrase, called a *mantra*.

Making a Marigold Garland

YOU WILL NEED:

- marigold flowers
- a large needle
- strong thread
- scissors

WHAT TO DO:

1 Pinch off the marigold flower heads. You could also use roses, carnations, or any other small, sturdy flowers.

2 Cut a length of thread about 4 feet long. Thread the needle.

3 Push the needle through the center of each flower head to thread it onto the string.

4 Tie the ends of the thread with a firm knot. Your garland is now ready to wear — or to offer to a god.

Although Hindus do not have one holy book (such as the Christian Bible) they have many sacred writings. Long before these texts were written down, they were passed on by word of mouth. The language used was *Sanskrit*, the language of the Aryan people (see page 4) and the sacred language of India. Sanskrit is still studied in India, but it is not used in everyday life.

THE VEDAS

The most ancient sacred texts are the *Vedas* – four collections of hymns, prayers, and rules for rituals and sacrifices. These were written down by the Aryans some 3,500 years ago. The oldest and best-known is the *Rig Veda*. It is still one of Hinduism's most important holy books. It contains more than a thousand hymns in praise of ancient gods and goddesses.

Many Hindus read and study the sacred books as part of their worship and use them as guides in their lives. Priests read from the sacred books at weddings and other ceremonies.

THE UPANISHADS

The *Upanishads* were compiled some 2,500 years ago. They deal with the relationship between Brahman and the individual soul, called *atman* (see page 7). They use stories and parables to discuss eternity and the soul. More than a hundred *Upanishads* have now been written down.

EPIC POEMS

Among the holy books of Hinduism are two great poems, the *Mahabharata* and the *Ramayana*.

The *Mahabharata* tells the story of two rival families – the *Kauravas* and *Pandavas* – who are fighting for control of the kingdom of Hastinapura. The most important part of the *Mahabharata* is the *Bhagavad Gita*, the "Song of the Lord." There, Krishna reminds *Arjuna*, one of the Pandavas, that each person must do their duty selflessly in order to gain salvation.

The *Ramayana* is the story of how Rama rescues his wife, Sita, from the demon king, *Ravana*, helped by his faithful friend, Hanuman (the monkey god). After many

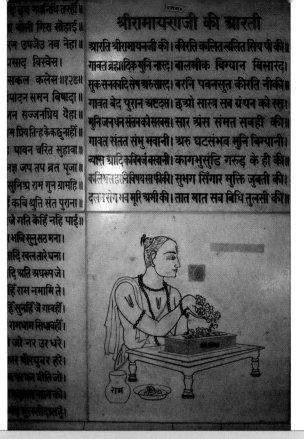

This is a passage from the *Ram Charit Manas*, a very famous version of the *Ramayana* poem, carved on a temple wall.

adventures, they complete their task, and Rama and Sita return in triumph to their home in *Ayodhya*. There they are crowned king and queen.

SPOTLIGHT

- The *Puranas* are ancient Sanskrit verses about the lives of the gods, kings, and saints.

- The name *Rig Veda* means "Song of Knowledge."

- *Sutras* are collections of sayings and snippets of information dealing with all aspects of life.

KRISHNA AND THE SERPENT KING

From an early age, Hindu children hear stories about the adventures of Krishna. The following tale comes from the *Bhagavata Purana*, a collection of stories about Krishna's life.

Kaliya, the serpent king, lived in the darkest depths of the River Yamuna. He had five heads for spitting poison, and he was so huge he could crush a person to death. Kaliya had spit so much poison into the river that any animal or person who drank the water died instantly. Now no one dared go near the river, for fear of being snatched by the serpent. Something had to be done.

Krishna decided that it was up to him to save the river and his friends. So he dived into the water, climbed onto one of Kaliya's five heads, and began to dance. He danced and danced until the heads were crushed under his feet. When he got to the last head, he stopped.

"I will spare your life on one condition," Krishna told Kaliya. "Leave the river and flee to the sea where you can do no more harm." Kaliya was so grateful to have his life spared that he swam away as fast as he could. The serpent king was never seen again. The river was left in peace once more.

PILGRIMS AND HOLY PLACES

Each year, millions of Hindus make pilgrimages, or *yatras*, to holy places connected with the gods or religious events. They may visit the great temples in the seven sacred cities, or *tirthas*, of India. These cities are Varanasi, Hardwar, Mathura, Ayodhya, Ujjain, Dwarka, and Kanchipuram. Hindus do not have to make pilgrimages but many feel that it brings them closer to moksha.

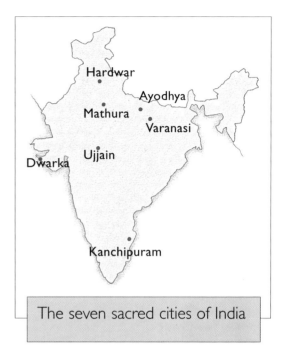

The seven sacred cities of India

VARANASI

Varanasi is the holiest of the seven tirthas. The city lies on the banks of the sacred River Ganges in northern India. Hindus believe that Varanasi was chosen by Shiva as his home on earth. Millions of pilgrims flock to Varanasi to bathe in the river and to visit the temples. Many elderly Hindus visit Varanasi because it is considered a particularly favorable place to die.

The steps leading down to the river at Varanesi are crowded with bathers, priests, temples, and sacred cows.

At Kumbh Mela celebrations people bathe in the river and collect jars of sacred river water to take home with them.

THE SACRED GANGES

To Hindus, the water of the River Ganges is sacred. They believe that bathing in the Ganges washes away their sins. The Ganges flows from the Himalaya Mountains, across northern India, to the Bay of Bengal in the east. According to legend, the Ganges fell to earth from heaven. Shiva caught the river in his hair to break its fall and prevent its weight from shattering the earth. The river is also worshiped as a goddess, called Ganga.

THE KUMBH MELA FAIR

Every twelve years, millions of pilgrims gather in the city of Allahabad. This is where the rivers Ganges and Yamuna meet the mythical Saraswati River. The actual meeting point, or *sangam*, is the site of the great *Kumbh Mela* fair, where people come to bathe in the waters of the holy rivers. A huge temporary town is built to accommodate the pilgrims.

SACRED MOUNTAINS

Mountains are special places, too. Mount Kailash in the Himalaya is sacred as the home of Shiva and Parvati. The Sri Amarnath cave in the Himalaya is also sacred to Shiva. At the time of the full moon in July-August, thousands of pilgrims make the long trek to worship at the cave.

No one can escape a drenching at Holi! Students drench their teachers, children drench their parents – just for one day.

Hundreds of Hindu festivals are held throughout the year. Some are national festivals celebrated in India and by Hindus living abroad. Others are local village celebrations. The festivities may include performing puja, wearing new clothes, exchanging gifts, eating special food, singing, dancing, and visiting relatives.

HOLI

The colorful festival of Holi marks the end of winter. On the night before Holi, bonfires are built to burn models of the witch named Holika. According to legend, Holika tried to kill her nephew because he worshiped Vishnu, but Holika was killed instead. On the day of Holi, people dress up in old clothes and drench each other with colored powder and water. It's great fun but very messy! In the evening, people visit their relatives and bring gifts of candy. Holi is also a special festival for farmers. They celebrate the first harvest of spring.

DIWALI

Diwali is the festival of lights, and it is celebrated over five days. People decorate their houses and temples with small lamps called *divas*. These are believed to light the hero Rama home to Ayodhya after his victory over Ravana (see page 19). There is a fireworks display in every town and village. Diwali is also dedicated to *Lakshmi*, the goddess of wealth, and marks the start of the Hindu New Year.

Hindus all over the world celebrate Diwali. These children in Britain are lighting the diva lamps.

DUSSEHRA

The festival of *Dussehra* lasts for ten days. In some places, it is known as *Ram Lila*. Plays are performed telling the story of Rama's life, and huge models of Ravana are burned. In other places, the festival is called

At the end of the Ram Lila play, a flaming arrow is fired at the model of Ravana, setting it on fire.

Durga Puja and celebrates Durga's victory over the buffalo-headed demon, Mahishasura.

THE HINDU YEAR

The Hindu religious calendar has twelve months, based on the phases of the moon. Each month runs from full moon to full moon and is divided into a light half and a dark half. In everyday life, however, Hindus use the same calendar as we do.

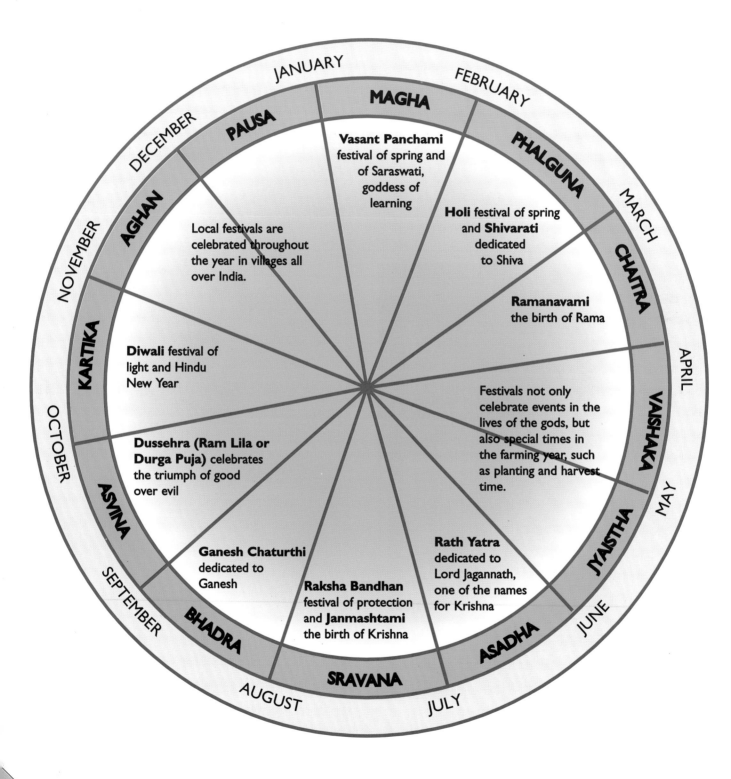

JANUARY
FEBRUARY
MARCH
APRIL
MAY
JUNE
JULY
AUGUST
SEPTEMBER
OCTOBER
NOVEMBER
DECEMBER

MAGHA
PHALGUNA
CHATRA
VAISHAKA
JYAISTHA
ASADHA
SRAVANA
BHADRA
ASVINA
KARTIKA
AGHAN
PAUSA

Vasant Panchami festival of spring and of Saraswati, goddess of learning

Holi festival of spring and **Shivarati** dedicated to Shiva

Ramanavami the birth of Rama

Festivals not only celebrate events in the lives of the gods, but also special times in the farming year, such as planting and harvest time.

Rath Yatra dedicated to Lord Jagannath, one of the names for Krishna

Raksha Bandhan festival of protection and **Janmashtami** the birth of Krishna

Ganesh Chaturthi dedicated to Ganesh

Dussehra (Ram Lila or Durga Puja) celebrates the triumph of good over evil

Diwali festival of light and Hindu New Year

Local festivals are celebrated throughout the year in villages all over India.

How to Make a Rakhi Bracelet

The festival of *Raksha Bandhan* takes place on the day of the full moon in the month of Sravana (July-August). Girls tie bracelets, called *rakhis*, around their brothers' wrists for protection. In return, brothers give their sisters gifts – usually of money. Try making your own rakhi bracelets.

YOU WILL NEED:
- glue
- tinsel
- cardboard
- ribbon or thick thread
- colored glitter, sequins, or small beads
- a penny
- scissors

WHAT TO DO:

1 Cut a small circle out of the cardboard. Trace around a coin to get the right shape.

3 Glue the ribbon or thread across the back of the cardboard circle.

2 Cut a piece of ribbon or thick thread to make the bracelet. Make sure the ribbon or thread is big enough to go around your wrist.

4 Decorate the circle with tinsel, glitter, or sequins. Or you can glue on tiny beads.

27

FAMILY CELEBRATIONS

The priest casts a horoscope at the time of a baby's birth. It will be consulted later to fix a good wedding date.

Family life is very important to Hindus. In India, several generations of a family often live together in the same house and help each other. Hindus who have settled in other countries continue to respect family ties, and celebrations remain very important to them. There are many special celebrations in a Hindu's life. These are usually a time for the whole family to get together.

CELEBRATING A BIRTH

When a baby is born to a Hindu family, a priest performs a special ceremony and says prayers for the good health and well-being of the mother and the baby. Ten days after the baby's birth, a naming ceremony takes place and the baby's horoscope is cast, showing the positions of the stars and planets at the time of the infant's birth.

THE SACRED THREAD

For boys from the top three castes, the most important ceremony of their childhood takes place when they are between nine and eleven years old. This is when they receive their sacred thread from the priest.

SPOTLIGHT

Hindu names all have a special meaning.
- Ram - the name of the god
- Raj - king
- Anand - happiness
- Mahesh - another name for Shiva
- Devi - goddess
- Deepika - light

They must wear these throughout their lives, looped over the left shoulder and under the right arm. This marks a new stage in a boy's life, when he begins to find out more about his religion and to take on more responsibility.

The priest prepares a young Hindu boy for his sacred thread ceremony, one of the most important times in his life.

DEATH AND CREMATION

When Hindus die, their bodies are cremated. In India, the body is placed on a pile of sandalwood logs. The logs are set on fire by the eldest son or eldest male relation. In other countries, the ceremony takes place in a crematorium. It is followed by twelve days of rites and ritual prayers for the dead person's soul. If possible, the dead person's ashes are sprinkled into the water of the River Ganges.

Hindus believe that when you are cremated, your body perishes in the fire but your soul lives on to be born again.

It takes a bride several hours to put on her wedding sari, makeup, and jewelry. Luckily, she has several helpers.

INTERVIEW

I come from Bihar in north central India but my parents arranged my marriage to a boy in England. My wedding took place in India, but I now live in England with my husband and our baby son.
Kamala Matilal, age 24. Oxford, England.

WEDDING DAY

Many Hindu weddings are arranged by the bride's and groom's parents. The wedding itself lasts for several days, with many rituals and ceremonies. The wedding can take place anywhere – at the bride's home, or in a special hall hired for the occasion. The bride wears special jewelry and a red silk *sari*. She sits with the groom in front of the sacred fire while the priest recites prayers and offers food to the gods. Then the bride and groom walk seven times around the fire to symbolize their marriage. After her wedding, the bride goes to live with her husband and his family.

Before her wedding, a bride's hands and feet are decorated with red *mehndi* patterns. The leaves of the mehndi, or henna, plant are crushed to form a paste and painted onto the bride's skin. After a few hours, the dried paste is washed off, leaving the pattern behind.

A bride-to-be is having her hands decorated with mehndi for her wedding. It takes a lot of patience and skill.

30

MEHNDI HANDS

YOU WILL NEED:

- *some henna powder (available in stores that sell hair-care products)*
- *a few drops of oil* • *lemon juice*
- *a used matchstick* • *sugar*
- *paper* •*spoon* •*pencil* •*cotton wool*

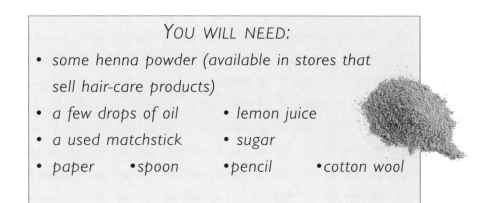

WHAT TO DO:

1 First, sketch out your pattern on a piece of paper. Try lots of different patterns. Then dab your friend's hand with lemon juice and sugar on cotton wool. This is to make the mixture stick.

2 Mix some of the henna powder with the oil and lemon juice to form a thick paste.

3 Then use the matchstick and henna paste to draw the pattern.

4 Leave the paste to dry for 2-3 hours. Then scrape it off carefully. The pattern will last for several days.

GLOSSARY

Aryans people from Central Asia who invaded northwest India in c.1,500 B.C. Their religion laid the foundations for Hinduism.

Brahman the supreme spirit of Hinduism.

caste a large group, or class, of people. In Hindu society, there are four main castes.

cremation the ritual of burning the body to ashes after a person has died.

divinity a god or goddess.

eternity forever.

halva a sweet dish made with nuts or carrots; eaten during many Hindu celebrations and festivals.

horoscope a chart drawn up to show the position of the stars and planets at the time of a person's birth; used for predicting a person's future life.

incense sweet-smelling fragrance burned in temples.

karma one's actions and their effects on others.

moksha ultimate freedom or salvation from samsara; being at one with Brahman.

pilgrimage a journey to an important religious place to pray or give thanks.

puja a common form of Hindu worship.

Ramayana one of the most sacred Hindu texts; tells the story of the god, Rama, and his wife, Sita.

reincarnation the belief that a person's soul is reborn into a different body when that person dies.

Rig Veda the oldest and one of the holiest Hindu texts.

Sanskrit the ancient, sacred language of Hinduism.

sari a style of dress worn by Indian women.

shrine part of a temple or a place of worship in a home, village or field.

samsara the cycle of birth, death and rebirth central to Hindu beliefs.

INDEX